The Secret of a Mommy's Love

By Ellen Krohne

The author has designated proceeds from the sale of this book to be donated to Heartlinks Grief Center.
To learn more about Heartlinks Grief Center, visit
www.myheartlinks.com

In loving memory of Doris Krohne, a wonderful mother, grandmother and sharer of the secret of a mommy's love.

"It is sure fun having all five grandchildren here while the kids are on their trip," said Grandpa Bill as he swept the floor. "And busy!" said Grandma Yellow. "It'll be more hectic when the new baby gets here. Ab and Crystal will soon be as busy as Russ and Joy were when they had their third, Quinn."

Benny was coloring with his cousin, Quinn. He frowned when he heard Grandma Yellow talk about the new baby. Mommy and Daddy talked all the time about this new baby. And they were always busy getting pink things for this new baby. Benny wasn't so sure he was going to like her, this new Baby Abigail.

Benny asked Quinn, "Will Mommy still love me when Baby Abigail gets here? Will she have enough love for me, too?" Quinn scrunched up her face and said, "I don't know. My mommy seems to have plenty for me, Ellie and Lincoln."

"I will help you find out, Benny," Quinn said, giving him a hug.

Benny and Quinn ran to find Bill and Ellie. "They are bigger, they will know," said Benny, smiling. "We have an important question!" they shouted. Ellie said, "SHHH! We are in school. Go out!"

Benny backed up so quickly he knocked Quinn over. Benny helped her up and she said, "Let's ask Lincoln. He is the oldest of us all. He is ten already. He will know about a mommy's love."

They ran down the stairs. "Lincoln, Lincoln, we need to ask you a question," said Benny. "Will my mommy have enough love for me once Baby Abigail gets here?"

Lincoln paused the game he was playing. "I am sure she will. My mommy did when we got Quinn. But I don't know how she gets more love, or where it comes from. That's a good question," he said.

Just then Bill and Ellie ran into the bedroom. "School's all done," said Ellie. "What is the important question?" Bill asked.

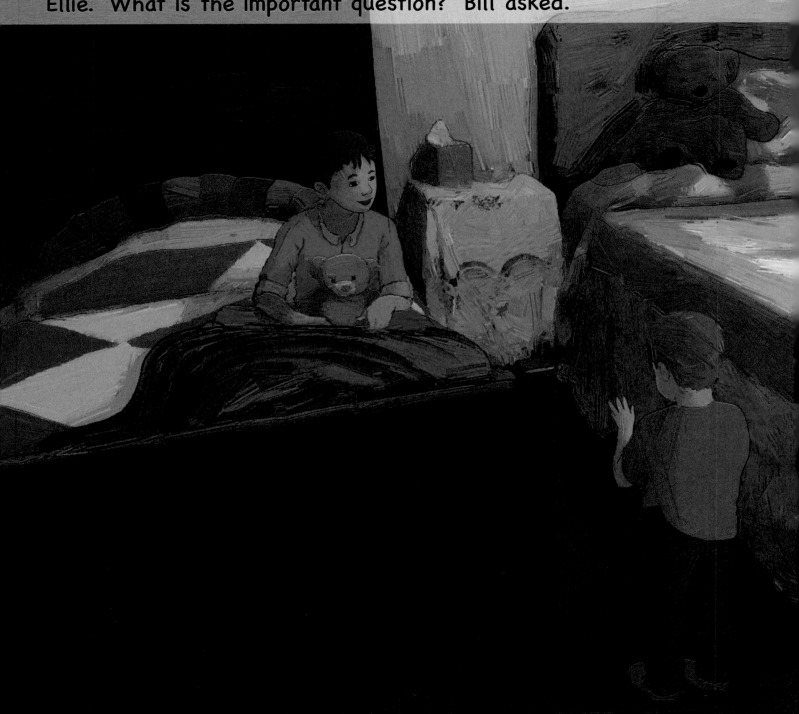

"Brother, will Mommy have enough love for me when Baby Abigail gets here?" Benny asked Bill, his lower lip shaking.

Bill thought for a minute and then said, "I know, I know this. Mommy will get superpowers when Baby Abigail gets here, like Wonder Woman! She will become 'Super-Mommy,' and her heart will grow so big that she will have plenty of love for all of us, Benny."

Ellie shouted, "Oh, wait, wait, I have an idea! Maybe your mommy will get sprinkled with fairy dust from the Magical Mommy Love Fairy that makes mommies' love grow and grow and grow and grow!"

Benny and Quinn were not so sure about those ideas. "Maybe we should ask Grandma Yellow and Grandpa Bill. They are really old. They will know," said Quinn.

They all ran up the stairs, where Grandma Yellow was setting the meal on the table. "Come, kids, let's say our meal prayer," Grandpa Bill said. "But we have an important question," they all said together. "Prayers first," said Grandma Yellow.

They made their circle like they always did. Grandpa Bill and
Grandma Yellow surrounded them in a big sandwich hug while they
sang, "Come Lord Jesus be our guest, let thy gifts to us be blessed."
Then they shouted as loud as they could, "AMEN!" Except Benny.
He didn't sing or shout.

"Now, now, can we ask the question?" Ellie asked, jumping up and down.

"Yes, sit down and ask away," said Grandpa Bill. "Will Mommy have enough love for me when Baby Abigail gets here?" Benny asked, his eyes brimming with tears.
"Don't worry, Benny, it will be all right," Bill said, giving his brother a warm look.

Grandpa Bill and Grandma Yellow smiled at each other. They remembered when their little girl, Joy, was waiting for her brother, Ab, and asked the same question.

"There is a secret we can share with you that my mother told us long ago," said Grandpa Bill.

"Are you ready?" asked Grandma Yellow.
            "When a new baby arrives,
            A mommy's love does not divide.
            It multiplies!"

"But what does it mean, divide, multiply?" cried Benny.

Lincoln said, "Benny, to divide means to split, like when we share a popsicle."

Bill said, "And to multiply means to grow, to get more."
"Like when Grandma Yellow adds bubbles to our bathtub, the
bubbles just grow and grow," said Ellie.

Benny and Quinn looked at each other. Quinn said, "But where does the extra love come from?" Grandma Yellow said, "Love is a special gift. When God brings a family a new baby, He also grows the mommy's love!"

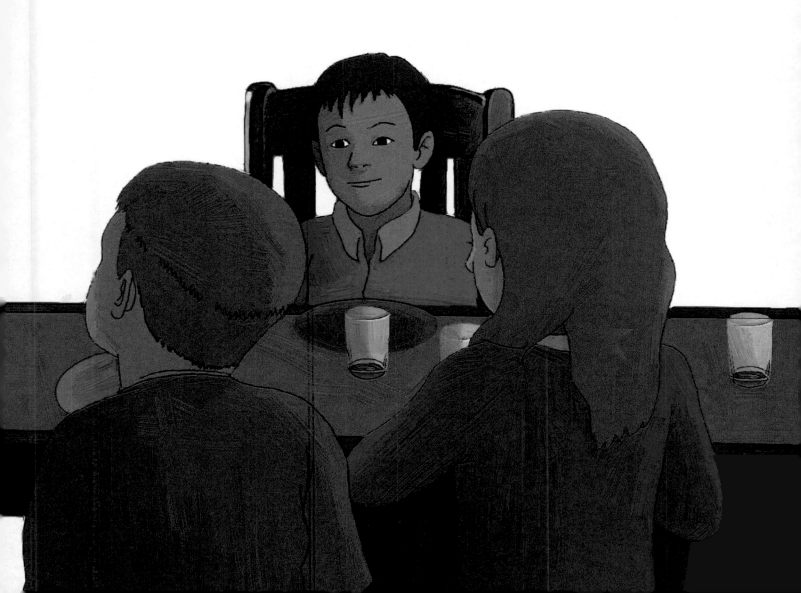

Benny started to cry. "How about Daddy's?" he asked. "Yes, yes, it works for daddies, too," said Grandpa Bill, patting Benny's arm.

"Hooray!" said Quinn and Benny together. They were excited and happy that they had solved the mystery.

Just then, all the parents came through the door, excited to see their little ones.

Benny patted his mommy's tummy and smiled. "I can't wait until Baby Abigail gets here!" he said. "We just learned the secret!"

"The secret?" Crystal asked. "Yes, yes, we all know the secret now,"
and they said together,
    "When a new baby arrives,
    A mommy's love does not divide.
    It multiplies!"

Joy winked at Ab. She remembered the secret their grandmother had shared with her long ago. "I am so happy that you all know the secret now," said Joy, smiling at her husband, Russ.

"Time for a big sandwich hug," said Ab. "And see, Mommy, there is plenty of room for Baby Abigail," said Benny, smiling.

Find Abby's Star

My grandchildren and I had fun taking the photo on the next page. After it was taken, I gathered them in my office for another book consultation.

I opened a book we cherished, **Goodnight Moon**. We'd searched for the hidden mouse on each page, called an Easter egg, many times.

They loved the idea of adding one to **The Secret of a Mommy's Love** and had some creative ideas of what to hide; an elephant, candy, a shark, a heart, a horsey. While we debated the ideas, Abby, now 16 months old, found my box of craft supplies. She spied a little bag of tiny gold stars and offered one to each of us. Lincoln looked at me and smiled, "Grandma, Abby picked our Easter egg!"

We all agreed, and hope you have fun finding Abby's star hidden on each page.

Love, Ellen

About the author:

Ellen Krohne is the award-winning author of **Heartbroken – Grief and Hope Inside the Opioid Crisis** and **We Lost Her** and is the grandmother of six. When her older grandchildren wanted to read her books (which are about grief) she said, "No, not till you are older." So, she wrote **The Secret of a Mommy's Love** in collaboration with her little ones. Ellen hopes you will enjoy the book and pass the special secret on to your family!

To learn more about the author, please visit: **www.ellenkrohne.com**

About the Illustrator:

Born in an Italian city called Livorno, Martina spent her childhood peeling her knees, falling down from the bike and drawing a lot, encouraged by her grandma who used to give her a lot of crayons! After she discovered a passion for comic books, she decided to study to become an illustrator in Firenze and later to move to the UK, Finland and Denmark where she is currently freelancing while drinking a lot of coffee.

Made in the USA
Monee, IL
12 April 2021